Personal Time Management

Third Edition

Marion E. Haynes

A Fifty-Minute™ Series Book

This Fifty-Minute™ book is designed to be "read with a pencil." It is an excellent workbook for self-study as well as classroom learning. All material is copyright-protected and cannot be duplicated without permission from the publisher. *Therefore, be sure to order a copy for every training participant by contacting:*

CRISP. Learning
Menlo Park, California

1-800-442-7477

CrispLearning.com

Personal Time Management

Third Edition

Marion E. Haynes

CREDITS:
Senior Editor: **Debbie Woodbury**
Editor: **Michael G. Crisp**
Copy Editor: **Charlotte Bosarge**
Production Manager: **Judy Petry**
Design: **Amy Shayne**
Production Artist: **Carol Lindahl, Darin Stumme**
Cartoonist: **Ralph Mapson**

© 1987, 1994, 2001 Crisp Publications, Inc.
Printed in the United States of America by Von Hoffmann Graphics, Inc.

CrispLearning.com

01 02 03 04   10 9 8 7 6 5 4 3 2 1

Library of Congress Catalog Card Number 00-106655
Haynes, Marion E.
Personal Time Management, Third Edition
ISBN 1-56052-585-1

This book is printed on recyclable paper with soy ink.

Learning Objectives For:

PERSONAL TIME MANAGEMENT

The objectives for *Personal Time Management, Third Edition* are listed below. They have been developed to guide you, the reader, to the core issues covered in this book.

THE OBJECTIVES OF THIS BOOK ARE:

❑ 1) To help you determine how you presently use time

❑ 2) To make you aware of the portion of time over which you have control

❑ 3) To teach you how to make the most effective use of the time under your control

❑ 4) To help you handle time not under your control in a more efficient way

❑ 5) To allow you to use time the way you choose (work, play, or rest)

ASSESSING YOUR PROGRESS

In addition to the learning objectives, CrispLearning has developed an **assessment** that covers the fundamental information presented in this book. A twenty-five item, multiple choice/true-false questionnaire allows the reader to evaluate his or her comprehension of the subject matter. An answer sheet with a chart matching the questions to the listed objectives is also available. To learn how to obtain a copy of this assessment please call: **1-800-442-7477** and ask to speak with a Customer Service Representative.

Assessments should not be used in any selection process.

Preface

The first edition of *Personal Time Management* enjoyed tremendous success. Over 100,000 copies were sold in the U.S., and it was republished in 11 other countries. The revised edition continued this success with sales over 225,000 copies, and the number of countries republishing the book has grown to 13. Audiocassettes, videocassettes, CD-ROMs, and video training packages based on the book are also available. This third edition saves all of the popular features of the prior editions and includes an expanded section on time-wasters plus an additional section on time-saving tips for the Internet.

This book contains cases studies, questionnaires, checklists, and exercises that reflect the material presented. Work through these as you go along, and they will serve as an excellent means of verifying your understanding and reinforcing your learning.

Better time management is within your grasp. If you are motivated to complete this book and apply the ideas it contains, you will gain from the experience.

Good luck!

Marion E. Haynes

Marion E. Haynes

Contents

Part 3: Time Management Innovations

Part 4: Time-Saving Tips for Travelers

Part 5: Action Planning

TYRANNY OF THE URGENT

Have you ever wished for a thirty-hour day? Surely this extra time would relieve the tremendous pressure under which we live. Our lives leave a trail of unfinished tasks. Unanswered letters, unvisited friends, unwritten articles, and unread books haunt quiet moments when we stop to evaluate.

But would a thirty-hour day really solve the problem? Wouldn't we soon be just as frustrated as we are now with our twenty-four allotment? A mother's work is never finished, and neither is that of any manager, student, teacher, or anyone else we know.

When we stop to evaluate, we realize that our dilemma goes deeper than shortage of time; it is basically the problem of priorities. Hard work does not hurt us. We know what it is to go full speed for long hours, and the resulting weariness is matched by a sense of achievement. Not hard work, but doubt and misgiving produce anxiety as we review a month or year and become oppressed by the pile of unfinished tasks. Demands have driven us onto a reef of frustration. We confess, quite apart from our sins, "we have left undone those things which we ought to have done; and we have done those things which we ought not to have done."

Several years ago an experienced manager said to me, "Your greatest danger is letting the urgent things crowd out the important." He didn't realize how hard his maxim hit. It often returns to haunt and rebuke me by raising the critical problem of priorities.

We live in constant tension between the urgent and the important. The problem is that the important task rarely must be done today, or even this week. The urgent task calls for instant action–endless demands, pressure every hour and day.

Even a home is no longer a castle; no longer a place away from urgent tasks because the telephone breaches the walls with imperious demands. The momentary appeal of new distractions seems irresistible and important, and they devour our energy. But in the light of time's perspective their deceptive prominence fades; and with a sense of loss we recall important tasks we have pushed aside. We realize we've become slaves to the "tyranny of the urgent."

Edited from Tyranny of the Urgent, *by Dr. Charles E. Hummell (Downers Grove, IL: InterVarsity Press,* © *1967). Used by permission of the publisher.*

Time Management

Principles

4

The Basics of Time Management

Time is a unique resource. Day to day, everyone has the same amount. It cannot be accumulated. You can't turn it on or off. It can't be replaced. It has to be spent at the rate of sixty seconds every minute.

Time management—like the management of other resources—benefits from analysis and planning. To understand and apply time management principles, you must know not only how you use time, but also what problems you encounter in using it wisely and what causes them. From this base you can learn to improve your effectiveness and efficiency through better time management.

Time management is a personal process and must fit your style and circumstances. It takes a strong commitment to change old habits; however, this choice is available and yours for the taking. If you choose to apply the principles in this book, you will obtain the rewards that come from better time investment.

The questionnaire on the following page will assist you in looking at your current time management attitudes and practices. It will help you identify the things you will want to concentrate on as you complete this book.

6

WE ALL GET 168 HOURS PER WEEK, HOW DO YOU USE YOURS?

Place a check (✔) in the column that best describes how you feel or act. Then review your responses and focus on each item to see if it represents an opportunity to improve your management of time.

		Usually	Sometimes	Rarely
1.	Do you normally spend time the way you really want to?	❑	☑	❑
2.	Do you often feel harried and obligated to do things you really don't want to do?	☑	❑	❑
3.	Do you feel a sense of accomplishment from your work?	☑	❑	❑
4.	Do you regularly work longer hours than your colleagues?	☑	❑	❑
5.	Do you regularly take work home on evenings or weekends?	☑	❑	❑
6.	Do you feel stress because of too much work?	☑	❑	☑
7.	Do you feel guilty about your performance at work?	☑	❑	☑
8.	Do you consider your job to be fun?	❑	❑	☑
9.	Can you find blocks of uninterrupted time when you need to?	❑	❑	❑
10.	Do you feel in control about the way you use your time?	❑	☑	❑
11.	Do you maintain a regular exercise program?	☑	❑	❑
12.	Do you take vacations or long weekends as often as you would like?	❑	☑	❑
13.	Do you put off doing the difficult, boring, or unpleasant parts of your job?	☑	❑	❑
14.	Do you feel you must always be busy doing something productive?	☑	❑	❑
15.	Do you feel guilty when you occasionally goof off?	❑	❑	☑

Adapted from Successful Time Management *by Jack D. Ferner, pp. 6-7 (NY: John Wiley & Sons, 1980). Used by permission of the publisher.*

What Controls Your Time?

The best starting place to improve your use of time is to determine the extent to which you control the time available to you. No one has total control over a daily schedule. Someone or something will always make demands. However, everyone has some control—and probably more than they realize.

A portion of each day (working hours or school hours) is regulated and should be used for those activities. Even within this structured time, there are opportunities to select which tasks or activities to handle and what priority to assign to each of them. It is the exercise of these discretionary choices that allows you to control your time.

CONTROL OF YOUR TIME

As an employee, your scheduled work hours should be used in pursuit of company objectives. In school, your time should be spent attending classes, studying, and learning. To this extent, your time is often controlled by specific tasks or assignments. However, several degrees of freedom usually exist in any specific time period. Where are you? (Circle one of the numbers below.)

Most Control   10   9   8   7   6   5   4   3   2   1   **Least Control**

Tasks or activities that allow personal control of my time	Tasks or activities that limit personal control of my time
_____	_____
_____	_____
_____	_____
_____	_____
_____	_____
_____	_____
_____	_____
_____	_____
_____	_____
_____	_____
_____	_____
_____	_____
_____	_____

Three Tests of Time

Analyzing how you presently use time is the first step to achieving better control of it. You must have specific, reliable information before you can determine opportunities for improvement. The best way to gather information is to keep a daily time log. Instructions and a form for such a log are provided on pages 100-101.

After this information has been recorded, you should examine it from three points of view: Necessity, Appropriateness, and Efficiency. This should allow you to discontinue certain tasks, delegate others, and find ways to increase efficiency through technology, new procedures, or personal work habits.

A careful analysis can often earn you another eight to 10 hours each week to spend on activities of your choice.

1 **The Test of Necessity:** First you should scrutinize each activity to be sure it is necessary—not just nice, but necessary. It is common to do things past their usefulness (e.g., monthly reports where the information is no longer used). This test of necessity should help reduce your tasks to the essential elements.

2 **The Test of Appropriateness:** Once the essential tasks have been identified, the next step should determine who should perform them (i.e., appropriateness in terms of department or skill level). There are probably activities that could be given to others. You may also find you are doing work beneath your skill level that can be easily reassigned.

3 **The Test of Efficiency:** The third analysis examines tasks that are remaining. Once you are satisfied that the work you are doing is necessary, ask yourself, "Is there a better way?" This will encourage you to find a faster way, by using better technology or establishing better procedures to handle recurring activities.

Although the examples described in this book are basically from the business world, similar principles apply to other aspects of your life.

ANALYZE FOR EFFECTIVE TIME UTILIZATION

In your own words, and from your own situation, list opportunities for more effective use of your time using the three tests described on page 9.

The Test of Necessity:

_____

_____

_____

The Test of Appropriateness:

_____

_____

_____

The Test of Efficiency:

_____

_____

_____

There Are Only Three Ways to Make Better Use of Your Time:

1. Discontinue low-priority tasks or activities.

2. Be more efficient at what you do.

3. Find someone else to take some of your work.

Benefits of Better Time Utilization

When you are able to make better use of time, you can benefit from activities such as:

➤ **CAREER PLANNING:** Set a course for your future and lay out a plan to achieve it. Move to a proactive mode and take charge of your own destiny.

➤ **READING:** Staying current is increasingly important in today's complex world. More time will allow you to read job-related materials, study new subjects, or learn more about a leisure activity.

➤ **COMMUNICATING:** Extra time will allow you to improve and initiate interpersonal relationships.

➤ **RELAXING:** You need to plan time for relaxation. When you do not take time off from the daily grind, your health may suffer or you may "burn out."

➤ **THINKING:** Improved methods and new opportunities come about as a result of innovation. More time will allow you to develop strategies and think through plans to establish and achieve significant new challenges.

CASE STUDY: LEARN THROUGH EXPERIENCE

Three months ago, Sheila looked forward to her promotion to supervisor. After four years in the department, she was confident of her abilities and knew her staff was capable and experienced.

Today, Sheila isn't so sure she was cut out to be a supervisor. There seems to be no end to her workday. During office hours her day is filled assigning work and reviewing results. Also, there is a steady flow of visitors, and the phone rings constantly. In the evening when she would like to relax, she has to take care of administrative matters such as reading mail, answering letters, preparing budgets, and completing performance appraisals.

In frustration, Sheila asked her friend Carol to join her for lunch. Sheila said she had something important to talk about. At lunch, she told Carol she was thinking about giving up her supervisor's job. She said she just couldn't face a lifetime of working 60 hours a week. Carol listened and then said there might be another way. If the only issue was the time required to the job, perhaps a review of how Sheila was using her time might help.

After listening to Sheila describe a typical week, Carol asked the following questions:

➤ Since she described her staff as capable and experienced, why was Sheila spending so much time assigning work and reviewing results?

➤ Who were the drop-in visitors? Could some be screened out?

➤ Could the department secretary take phone calls and refer some to others or have non-urgent calls returned at a more convenient time?

➤ Could some of Sheila's work be done by someone else?

With those thoughts in mind, Sheila returned to her office with a commitment to take a closer look at her use of time.

CONTINUED

Consider Sheila's situation and answer the following questions.

1. Does she appear to be making effective use of delegation?

    ❑ yes ❑ no

2. If her visitors are employees, how might she avoid interruptions?

    _____

    _____

3. Should Sheila consider establishing a "quiet time" when she would receive no calls or visitors? If so, when might be the best time of day?

    _____

    _____

4. Sheila feels she should assign all departmental work and review all results. Is there a more efficient way?

    _____

    _____

5. In what other ways could Sheila gain more control over her use of time?

    _____

    _____

HOW WOULD YOU HANDLE THESE SITUATIONS?

Listed below are situations where an opportunity exists to improve the use of time. Read each example and then check (✔) the choice you feel is the best response.

1. As Jean reviews time cards each week, she spends two hours summarizing the hours of employees who have exceptions such as sick relief or vacation time. She is aware that the payroll department gathers this same information and provides it to all department heads. What should she do?

❑ A. Continue summarizing the information.

❑ B. Stop summarizing the information.

❑ C. Point out the duplication to her supervisor and request permission to stop doing to work.

2. John likes to interview job candidates. He is excellent at matching candidates with job openings. Now that John is manager, he still spends about five hours a week interviewing even though he has a staff to handle this work. As a result, he often takes work home. What should John do?

❑ A. Stay with his present practice. He's the manager and has the right to do as he wishes.

❑ B. Delegate some of the administrative work to his staff so that he can keep interviewing.

❑ C. Stop interviewing except when the workload exceeds his staff's capacity.

CONTINUED

3. When Alexis assumed her present job, she noticed the quality of expense summaries she received from accounting was inadequate. Expenses were incorrectly allocated, and often two months passed before accounts were correct. In order to have timely, accurate information, Alexis now spends six hours a week keeping her own records. What should she do?

❑ **A. Continue keeping her own records. It is the only way to know they will be done correctly.**

❑ **B. Stop keeping her own records and use what the accounting department furnishes.**

❑ **C. Meet with the accounting department to work out a way to get the information she needs.**

4. Patrick is an assistant in the personnel department. Several times each month, employees ask him to work up an estimate of their retirement benefits. He does them by hand, and each estimate takes 45 minutes. What should Patrick do?

❑ **A. Continue his present practice, it seems to work okay.**

❑ **B. Refuse to prepare estimates except for employees planning to retire within one year.**

❑ **C. Develop and produce a computer-generated summary sheet which can be personalized.**

5. Carlos distributes a computer-generated report to field offices quarterly. A couple of his field colleagues told him that they don't use the report. What should he do?

❑ **A. Ignore the comments and continue to distribute the report.**

❑ **B. Stop distributing the report and see what happens.**

❑ **C. Survey all field offices and recommend a change in the report based on what is found.**

6. Janice receives 25 to 40 inquiries daily from members about the association's medical insurance coverage. Each one demands a personal reply. This part of her job consumes most of her time, leaving little time for her other duties. What should she do?

❑ **A. Continue providing personal service to members—they are entitled to it.**

❑ **B. Develop a form letter and mail it along with a plan summary in response to all inquiries.**

❑ **C. Study recent inquiries to see what questions are most recently asked and develop a series of replies on the word processor that can be personalized.**

The author feels that "C" is best in all situations.

Prime Time

When considering a daily schedule, it is a good idea to keep your energy cycle in mind. Some people are at their best early in the morning. Others peak in the afternoon. Whenever possible, try to plan your daily schedule to match your *prime time*. You will not always have control, but consider such ideas as doing work that requires concentration, creativity, and thought during your prime time. Leave less demanding activities, such as reading, responding to mail, or returning phone calls, until after lunch if your prime time is in the morning.

On the following page is an exercise to help you visualize your energy cycle.

Typical Energy Cycle

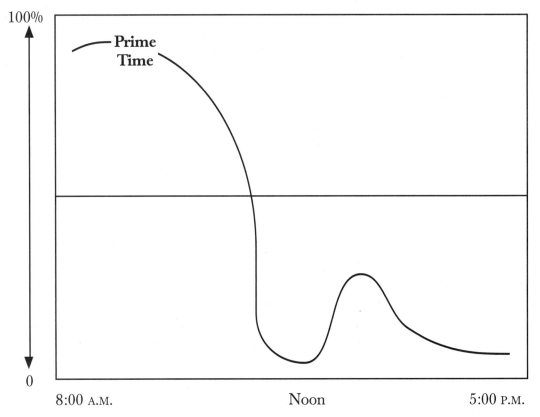

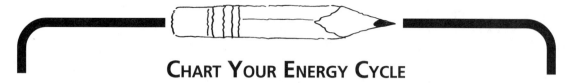

CHART YOUR ENERGY CYCLE

Fill in the beginning and ending time of your day on the following diagram. Then draw a line through the day, reflecting your typical energy cycle.

Typical Energy Cycle

100%

0

_____ A.M.   Noon   _____ P.M.

1. Do you arrange your workday or class load to take advantage of your energy cycle? ❑ yes ❑ no

2. What could you do differently to better utilize your period of peak energy?

_____

_____

_____

_____

Setting Priorities

When opportunities exceed resources, decisions must be made. Nowhere is this more apparent than in the use of time. Since time cannot be manufactured, you must decide what to do and what not to do.

Setting priorities in the use of time is a two-step process:

1. listing things that need to be done

2. prioritizing items on the list

The ABC Method

Use the *ABC Method* to determine your priorities by placing each item on your list into one of the following categories:

➤ **PRIORITY A** "Must Do"—these are the critical items. Some may fall into this category because of management directives, important customer requirements, significant deadlines, or opportunities for success or advancement.

➤ **PRIORITY B** "Should Do"—these are items of medium value. Items in this category may contribute to improved performance but are not essential or do not have critical deadlines.

➤ **PRIORITY C** "Nice to Do"—this is the lowest-value category. While interesting or fun, they could be eliminated, postponed, or scheduled for slack periods.

Your A's, B's, and C's are flexible, depending on the date your list is prepared. Priorities change over time. Today's B may become tomorrow's A as an important deadline approaches. Likewise, today's A may become tomorrow's C if it does not get accomplished in time or circumstances change.

Obviously, it is not worthwhile to spend considerable time on a task of modest value. On the other hand, a project of high value is worth the time invested. Only good planning will allow you to reap the benefits of time wisely invested. Use the form on page 21 to practice setting priorities.

MY PRIORITIES
FOR THE WEEK OF: _____

PRIORITY A–MUST DO

_____
_____
_____
_____
_____
_____
_____

PRIORITY B–SHOULD DO

_____
_____
_____
_____
_____
_____
_____

PRIORITY C–NICE TO DO

_____
_____
_____
_____
_____
_____

This sheet may be copied for your use.

Criteria for Setting Priorities

➤ **JUDGMENT.** You are the best judge of what you have to do. Let the pang of guilt you feel from not getting something done sharpen your judgment.

➤ **RELATIVITY.** As you compare tasks or activities, it should become clear that some are higher priority than others. You should always be guided by the question, "What is the best use of my time right now?"

➤ **TIMING.** Deadlines have a way of dictating priorities. Also important, but often overlooked, is a required starting time in order to finish a project by its deadline.

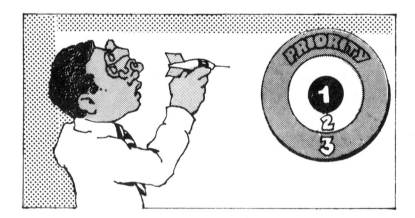

TWO EXTRA HOURS A DAY

If you had two extra hours each day, how would you use them? Answer by putting a check (✔) in front of each statement that applies. Add your own ideas.

- ❑ Do more planning
- ❑ Do more reading
- ❑ Spend some time on new work projects
- ❑ Spend more time with my family and friends
- ❑ Begin or expand an exercise program
- ❑ Spend more time on personal financial matters
- ❑ Start or expand a hobby
- ❑ Handle something I've been putting off

(Add your own)

- ❑ _____
- ❑ _____
- ❑ _____
- ❑ _____

REVIEW WORKSHEET

1. Following are ways I can make better use of my time:

    _____

    _____

    _____

    _____

2. The major roadblocks to a more effective and efficient use of my time are:

    _____

    _____

    _____

    _____

3. If I "found" five hours a week, here is how I would use that time:

    _____

    _____

    _____

    _____

4. The following activities involve a lot of my time, yet don't seem to contribute much to my objectives:

    1._____

    2._____

    3._____

    4._____

    5._____

How to Control Your Use of Time

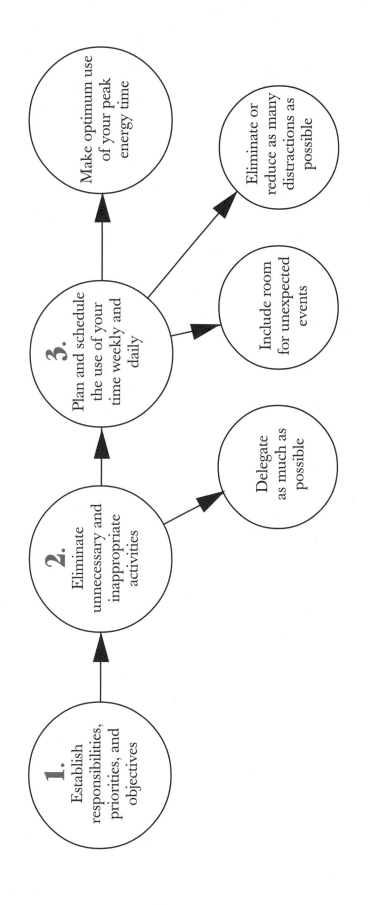

SELF-ASSESSMENT QUESTIONNAIRE

The following statements summarize the principles presented in Part 1 of this book. Check (✔) those that apply to you. Review items you did not check to see if an opportunity may exist for future efficiency.

- ❑ I know when my peak energy period occurs.

- ❑ I have adjusted my daily routine to make maximum use of my prime time.

- ❑ I have a written summary of my responsibilities.

- ❑ I have listed my objectives for the next quarter.

- ❑ I have prioritized my use of time.

- ❑ I have eliminated all unnecessary and inappropriate tasks.

- ❑ I have studied ways to improve efficiency in handling routine matters.

- ❑ I delegate whenever logical and possible.

- ❑ I prepare a daily "things to do" list.

- ❑ I leave some time for the unexpected each day.

- ❑ I realize that I can't do everything and must choose the best alternatives.

Time Management Techniques

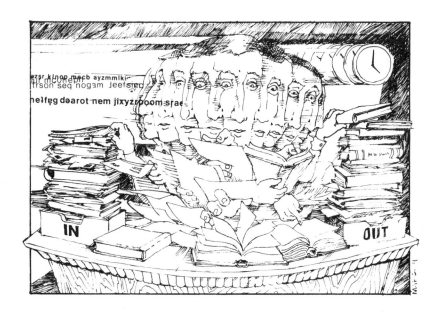

Planning

Planning is a complex process. Some people are good at it, others aren't. Some seem so caught up in activities and deadlines they claim there is no time to plan. Yet planning is the key to relieve the stress of too little time. It is the way to structure your future.

Planning makes two contributions which bring order to your life. First, it tells you how to get from where you are to where you want to be. Second, it identifies the resources required to get you there. Planning allows you to work on and complete a project on schedule, as well as estimate a cost more accurately.

Planning typically is either long-term or short-term. In this book, long-term plans describe what you expect to accomplish during the next three months as well as with any project whose duration exceeds a week. Short-term plans cover what you expect to accomplish today or this week, including steps toward longer-term objectives.

MY TIME FRAME

Long-Term Objectives: Following are my objectives for the next quarter, plus my projects that will take longer than a week to complete:

_____

_____

_____

_____

_____

_____

_____

Short-Term Goals: Following are those things that need doing this week including steps toward longer-term objectives:

_____

_____

_____

_____

_____

_____

_____

_____

Long-Term Planning Aids

Planning aids are a critical part of effective time management. It simply is not possible to remember everything. Four common planning aids are presented on the following pages:

>   **an Action-Planning Worksheet**

>   **a Milestone Chart**

>   **a PERT Diagram**

>   **a Master Calendar**

From these alternatives you can select the technique that best fits the type of work you do. Using a planning aid will help bring order to your life.

One word of caution—do not get too elaborate. Don't spend more time drawing and updating planning aids than is required. In other words, your planning should save you time, not *cost* you time.

Regardless of the technique you choose, your Master Calendar should record all activities. Note the due dates for each action step as well as project completion dates. When others are responsible for a step in your plan, ensure you have a follow-up date assigned. Also, always know who has responsibility for each step and the date the action is to be completed.

Action-Planning Worksheet

Action-Planning worksheets can vary greatly in complexity. The most simple show only those steps required to complete a project. Additional information on Action-Planning Worksheets can be beginning dates, targeted completion dates, cost estimates, and who is responsible for what task.

ACTION-PLANNING WORKSHEET

Objective: *Publish a Work Planning and Review workbook by May 31.*

Action Step	Est. Time	Target Date	Assigned Responsibility
1. Write draft	15 days	Apr. 15	Self
2. Type draft	10 days	Apr. 25	Secretary
3. Proofread	5 days	Apr. 20	Self & Secretary
4. Draw cover	5 days	Apr. 30	Graphics
5. Type final	10 days	May 10	Key entry
6. Proofread	3 days	May 13	Self & Secretary
7. Make corrections	2 days	May 15	Key entry
8. Draw figures	5 days	May 15	Graphics
9. Reproduce	15 days	May 30	Print shop
10. Deliver books		May 31	Print shop

ACTION-PLANNING WORKSHEET

Objective: _____

_____

_____

_____

| Action Step | Target Date | Cost | | Assigned Responsibility |
		Dollars	Time	

This sheet may be copied for your use.

Milestone Chart

A Milestone Chart graphically displays the relationship of the steps in a project. To create one, list the steps required to finish the project and estimate the time required for each step. Then list the steps down the left side of the chart, with dates shown along the bottom. Draw a line across the chart for each step, starting at the planned beginning date and ending on the completion date of that step. Once completed, you should be able to see the flow of the action steps and their sequence (including those that can be underway at the same time).

The usefulness of a Milestone Chart will be improved by also charting actual progress. This is usually done by drawing a line in a different color under the original line to show actual beginning and completion dates of each step.

Example

Objective: *Publish a Work Planning and Review workbook by May 31.*

Action Steps with Time Estimates:

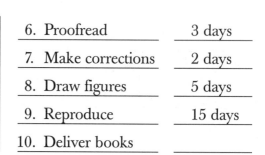

1. Write draft	15 days		6. Proofread	3 days
2. Type draft	10 days		7. Make corrections	2 days
3. Proofread	5 days		8. Draw figures	5 days
4. Draw cover	5 days		9. Reproduce	15 days
5. Type final	10 days		10. Deliver books	

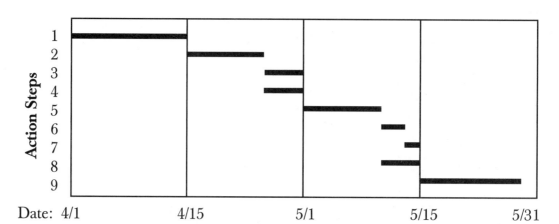

PRACTICE A MILESTONE CHART

Select a project and practice drawing a Milestone Chart.

Objective: _____

_____

_____

Action Steps with Time Estimates:

_____ _____   _____ _____

_____ _____   _____ _____

_____ _____   _____ _____

_____ _____   _____ _____

_____ _____   _____ _____

_____ _____   _____ _____

_____ _____   _____ _____

_____ _____   _____ _____

Action Steps

Dates

PERT Diagram

A PERT diagram represents an added degree of sophistication in the planning process. PERT stands for

➤ **P**rogram

➤ **E**valuation and

➤ **R**eview

➤ **T**echnique

To draw one, list the steps required to finish a project and estimate the time required to complete each step. Then draw a network of relationships among the steps. The number of the step is shown in a circle, and the time to complete the step is shown on the line leading to the next circle. Steps that must be completed in order are shown on one path to clarify proper sequencing. Steps that can be underway at the same time are shown on different paths.

A PERT Diagram not only shows the relationship among various steps in a project, but also serves as an easy way to calculate the critical path. The critical path is shown as a broken line in the example on the next page. It is the longest time path through the network and identifies essential steps that must be completed on time in order to not delay completion of the total project.

The usefulness of the PERT Diagram can be increased by coloring each step as it is completed. Actual time may be written over the estimated time to maintain a running tally of actual versus planned time along the critical path.

Example

Objective: _Publish a Work Planning and Review workbook by May 31._

Action Steps with Time Estimates:

1. Write draft	15 days	6. Proofread	3 days
2. Type draft	10 days	7. Make corrections	2 days
3. Proofread	5 days	8. Draw figures	5 days
4. Draw cover	5 days	9. Reproduce	15 days
5. Type final	10 days	10. Deliver books	

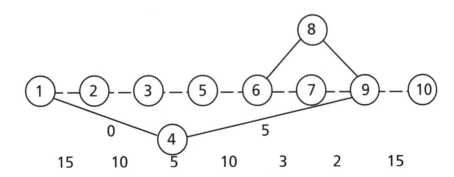

PRACTICE DRAWING A PERT DIAGRAM

Select a project and use it to practice drawing a PERT Diagram.

Objective: _____

_____

_____

Action Steps with Time Estimates:

_____ _____   _____ _____

_____ _____   _____ _____

_____ _____   _____ _____

_____ _____   _____ _____

_____ _____   _____ _____

_____ _____   _____ _____

_____ _____   _____ _____

_____ _____   _____ _____

Short-Term Planning Aids

Action steps in long-term plans must be integrated and prioritized with your other demands. These discrete steps become part of your short-term plans. Short-term plans are best developed and scheduled on both a weekly and a daily basis.

Weekly Plans

A weekly plan should describe what you want to accomplish by the end of the week and the activities required to get you there. Plans for the following week can be developed on Friday, over the weekend, or on Monday morning. (Many people use commuting time for this activity.)

Weekly worksheets may be simple or complex. The example on the following page can serve as a starting point for your short-term plans.

Once completed, your worksheet should be kept handy for frequent reference. Daily activities should be transferred to a daily calendar and take place according to an assigned priority.

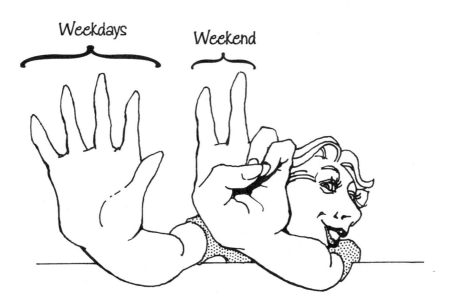

WEEKLY PLANNING WORKSHEET

For the week of: _____

Objectives:

1. _____

2. _____

3. _____

Activities	A/B/C Priority	Est. Time	Assigned Day

This sheet may be copied for your use.

Daily Plans

The culmination of the planning process is the best use of your time each day. If you make a habit of using a daily calendar, many of your activities will already be recorded. This is the best starting place to develop your list of "things to do today."

A daily, prioritized list is the best way to focus attention on your most important objectives. Work from the top of your list. If unexpected demands come up, assess their priority and handle them accordingly. Don't use something unexpected as an excuse to distract you. At the end of each day, review what was accomplished and carry forward any items on your list that need completing. Reprioritize these with tomorrow's new items.

The format for your list is not important. It can be written anywhere—on a calendar, a plain sheet of paper, or a form that you develop. Many stationery stores have a variety of planning forms available. The example below illustrates how simple a daily form can be. The example on the next page is more elaborate.

Use your "to do" list to lay out a daily schedule. It should reflect meetings and appointments, plus time to accomplish other priority items on your list.

Example

Things to Do Today
Make travel arrangements
Attend budget review @ 10:00 A.M.
Complete salary proposals
Reserve conference room for Wed.
Call insurance agent
Make dentist appointment

DAILY PLANNING WORKSHEET

Date:_____

Tasks to Complete	Done	Appointments to Keep
		7:00
		8:00
		9:00
		10:00
		11:00
		12:00
Phone Calls to Make	**Done**	
		1:00
		2:00
		3:00
People to See	**Done**	4:00
		5:00
		6:00
		7:00

This sheet may be copied for your use.

Conference Planner

Do you frequently need to communicate with co-workers for information to complete your work? Often this causes an interruption they may find distracting. One way to handle the situation efficiently is to use a Conference Planner (see example on the following page).

First, enter the names of those you frequently call on. Then, as you think of an item you need to discuss, note it under the person's name. When it is time to have a conference, prioritize the list. Cross out unimportant items or those that can be handled better in some other way.

CONFERENCE PLANNER

Name:	Name:	Name:
Name:	**Name:**	**Name:**
Name:	**Name:**	**Name:**

This sheet may be copied for your use.

Characteristics of Good Planners

The following statements describe how people view different aspects of planning. Check (✔) those statements that, in your opinion, reflect the views of a good planner.

❏ It is necessary to identify and operate within two time horizons. Anticipating events allows things that contribute to achieving long-term objectives to get done in the near term.

❏ An up-to-date Master Calendar can be your most helpful planning tool. However, detailed project plans must be developed before valid entries can be made on a Master Calendar.

❏ When things begin to get hectic, a "things to do today" list helps focus attention on the highest priority items.

❏ Action-Planning Worksheets, Milestone Charts, and PERT Diagrams are excellent planning aids when properly used.

❏ Planning contact with colleagues and staff will help minimize the disruption of their schedules. One way to do this is to use a Conference Planner.

❏ The most effective approaches to planning are those tailored to meet individual needs. Concepts, procedures, and worksheets are all subject to modification to fit individual circumstances.

CASE STUDY: ANOTHER DAY AT THE OFFICE

It was 7:20 A.M. when Myron arrived at the office. He was early because he wanted to clear the backlog of work that had been piling up on his desk. He turned on the lights and started to go through yesterday's mail. As he read the first piece, he realized he couldn't deal with it until a colleague arrived. He set it aside and went on to the next. This item had potential application to a project he was working on, so he walked down the hall and made a copy for his personal use.

As he continued reading his mail, he came across a journal article of particular interest and became engrossed in it. He was startled to find as he finished that others were arriving and it was nearly nine o'clock.

He quickly pushed the remaining mail to a corner of his desk and reached for a project file due tomorrow with at least two days' work yet to be completed. As he opened the file, Bill and Claire stopped by and invited him to join them for coffee. Myron decided he could spare ten minutes. Bill and Claire were both anxious to share the details of a play they had attended last night. Before Myron realized it, 30 minutes had passed, and he hurried back to his office.

As Myron entered his office, the phone rang. It was Mr. Wilson, his manager. There was a meeting scheduled at 10:00. Could Myron sit in for him? There was something to be discussed, about which the department should know. Myron looked at his watch. There wasn't enough time to get started on the project, so he pushed the file aside and vowed to start it immediately after lunch.

The afternoon wasn't any better. A few visitors, a few phone calls, a couple of letters and the day was over. Nothing had been accomplished on the project that was due tomorrow. As he stuffed the papers into his briefcase, he wondered how Bill and Claire were able to attend plays during the evening.

CONTINUED

CONTINUED

Examine Myron's use of time:

1. Did he make good use of prime time? ❑ yes ❑ no

2. Was he working on his highest priority task? ❑ yes ❑ no

3. Did he seem able to say no? ❑ yes ❑ no

4. Did he practice task completion? ❑ yes ❑ no

5. Does he seem to understand his problem? ❑ yes ❑ no

Common Time-Wasters

Everyone wastes time. It is part of being human. Some wasted time can be constructive, because it helps you to relax or otherwise reduce tension. Other wasted time, however, can be frustrating. This is especially true when time is wasted because you are doing something less important or less fun than what you might otherwise be doing.

The key question is, what else might you be doing that is of a higher personal priority? Taking a break, communicating with associates, talking on the telephone, and reading are not time-wasters unless they keep you from higher priority activities.

Time-wasters usually originate from two sources. One is your environment, and the other is yourself. Some typical examples of each are shown on the facing page.

The next few pages will concentrate on ways for you to recognize and manage your most frequent time-wasters.

Examples of Common Time-Wasters

Self-Generated Time-Wasters

If time is spent searching for misplaced items, or wasted due to distractions which cause you to start and stop several times before a task is completed, then you need to evaluate your work area.

Disorganization

Disorganization is a key culprit in wasted time. Evidence of disorganization shows up in the layout of a work area. Check it out. Is it efficient? Is it organized to minimize effort? Is there a free flow of materials and movement? Have you considered the placement of equipment such as telephone and computer, the proximity of supplies that are frequently used and your accessibility to active files?

Next, focus on your desk. Is your work area cluttered? How much time do you waste looking for things you know are there but can't find? When was the last time you used some of the items in and on your desk? Perhaps a housecleaning is in order.

The old axiom "A place for everything and everything in its place" is the best advice for organizing the information you need. Files should be set up for work in progress and kept handy. Everything relating to a particular project should be kept in one file folder. Files should be indexed for quick reference. Call-up procedures are required for items that need future action. A folder for current items received by mail, telephone, or visit should be maintained and checked daily to see what needs to be done.

Finally, organize your approach to work. Practice completing your tasks. If interrupted, do not immediately jump to a new task. Assess the priority of a request and avoid getting involved in any new activity until it becomes your top priority. If an interruption comes by phone or personal visit, simply return to the task you were working on as soon as the interruption ends.

How to Set Up a Personal Filing System

It is not necessary to be too logical. It is your system, and no one else will be using it, so it only needs to make sense to you.

Use a limited number of categories. For example, you may find the following five to be adequate:

1 **Projects:** In this category are individual files with information related to different projects you are working on.

2 **Instant Tasks:** This category should include folders on little jobs to fill in your time when you have a few minutes, perhaps low-priority letters to be answered, or general-interest articles.

3 **Self-Development:** This category contains folders related to training: books, articles, etc.

4 **Ideas:** This category contains items you wish to investigate further to improve your operation.

5 **Background Information:** This category is a resource for various things with which you are involved. Keep separate folders by topic and refer to them when you need statistics, examples, quotations, etc.

It may be a good idea to color code by priority within each category to draw attention to important items. This is easily accomplished by using different color highlighters and marking individual folders.

Keep your filing current so that time won't be wasted searching for an item.

Clean your files periodically to keep the volume of material to an essential minimum. This also will reduce time going through files when you are looking for something.

Procrastination

We all put things off. Typically, these items include boring, difficult, unpleasant or onerous tasks that ultimately need completing. When this happens to you, consider the following ideas:

➤ Set a deadline to complete the task and stick with it.

➤ Build in a reward system. For example, tell yourself, "When I finish that task I'm going to enjoy a nice meal with my special other." Or, "I won't go home until I finish this task."

➤ Arrange with someone (an associate, a secretary, etc.) to routinely follow up with you about progress on tasks you tend to put off.

➤ Do undesirable tasks early in the day so that you can be done with them.

Tips for Dealing with Procrastination

❏ Set a deadline

❏ Do it first

❏ Set up a reward system

❏ Break jobs into small pieces

❏ Arrange for follow-up

❏ Do it now!

Personal Needs

Many self-generated time-wasters are the result of efforts to satisfy personal needs such as social acceptance, perfection, and risk avoidance. Generally, people are unaware of this process. For example, it is most uncommon to hear someone say, "I have a high need for acceptance and therefore will do whatever you ask in order to satisfy that need." Rather, an individual takes on extra work, responds to every request, and feels good when others express appreciation. In the meantime, other, more important work is left undone. To take a cursory look at your needs profile, complete the Personal Needs Assessment Questionnaire on the following pages.

PERSONAL NEEDS ASSESSMENT

Indicate the extent to which you agree or disagree with each statement by entering one of these values.

5 = Completely agree   4 = Tend to agree   3 = Uncertain
2 = Tend to disagree   1= Completely disagree

_____   1. I could not work in a job that required me to work alone most, or all, of the time.

_____   2. What others think of me is extremely important to me.

_____   3. I worry about mistakes I've made in my work.

_____   4. I would be terribly embarrassed if someone found an error in my work.

_____   5. I prefer to be a member of a team rather than work alone.

_____   6. I am pleased when others ask me for assistance and I will do everything I can to comply.

_____   7. I am not satisfied until I have done my very best on any given task or assignment.

_____   8. I frequently spend a lot of time studying or analyzing possibilities before taking action.

_____   9. A friendly social atmosphere is an important part of a good place to work.

_____   10. I frequently subordinate my views and desires to those expressed by others.

_____   11. The only way to be sure something is done correctly is to do it yourself.

_____   12. Rules and regulations are to be understood and strictly followed.

_____   13. It is necessary, and appropriate, to take a portion of a workday for friendly conversation.

CONTINUED

CONTINUED

_____ 14. I find it difficult to end conversations even when they interfere with my work.

_____ 15. I often spend a lot of time correcting or redoing work done by others.

_____ 16. I prefer a lot of organization and structure in my job.

_____ 17. I take a great deal of pride in the number of friends I have.

_____ 18. I often guess at what someone wants rather than be embarrassed by asking for more information.

_____ 19. People who turn out less-than-perfect quality of work are either careless or lazy.

_____ 20. I have a need to include the thoughts and wishes of others in decisions I make that might affect them.

SCORING

List your responses on the lines below that correspond to each statement. Add the values of your responses and record the total for each column.

Social Interaction	Acceptance	Perfection	Risk Avoidance
1. _____	2. _____	3. _____	4. _____
5. _____	6. _____	7. _____	8. _____
9. _____	10. _____	11. _____	12. _____
13. _____	14. _____	15. _____	16. _____
17. _____	18. _____	19. _____	20. _____

Totals:

_____ _____ _____ _____

A score of 16 or more indicates a high need. A score of 20 or more indicates a need sufficiently strong to be a potential problem in your effective use of time.

Needs Profile Analysis

Social Interaction

Many jobs provide adequate opportunity to satisfy social needs. However, other jobs do not. Problems can arise when people with high social needs occupy jobs with little built-in opportunity to satisfy those needs. When this occurs, needs are typically satisfied in non-productive ways.

People with unsatisfied high social needs tend to waste not only their time but also the time of others in close proximity. They tend to be drop-in visitors with no particular agenda—or a very superficial one. Having dropped in, their conversations often are difficult to terminate.

If you fall into this category, two ideas may help:

First, respect the time of others. Ask if he or she has time to talk or if it would be better for you to come back later. Observe your conversational partner. Does he or she seem anxious to do something else? Watch for such things as standing up and moving away, glancing at papers, or even returning to work by writing, typing at the keyboard, or making calculations.

Second, develop ways to have your social needs satisfied productively. Consider getting together with colleagues at lunch, scheduling breaks with others in advance, requesting assignments to ad hoc work teams, and getting involved in group activities after work.

Acceptance

Many work groups provide an adequate opportunity to satisfy high acceptance needs. The self-worth of individual group members is confirmed through normal interaction and feedback. This process is further enhanced when group members cooperate and support each other. They don't make unreasonable demands on one another, and they work together to minimize the impact of demands from outside the group.

People with unsatisfied high acceptance needs tend to take on too much work. They often are viewed as "easy" by others, and others, therefore, take advantage of them. Doing what others ask is the price paid for acceptance, confirmation of self-worth, and being liked. It is often a very high price in terms of alternate use of time. Time used responding to such requests may be wasted when it takes you away from higher-priority work.

If you score high in this category, the following ideas may help you gain better control over the use of your time:

First, look for ways to provide confirmation of worth. You can do this in two ways. As you address a task, determine the significance of the task and the contribution it can make to your organization. Then, give it your best effort. When you finish, reflect on and experience the pride of having completed the task and done it well. Be willing to figuratively pat yourself on the back. Do not depend solely on others for confirmation of your value.

Second, take inventory of the things you do well. Frequently, attention is focused on what is not done well, i.e., where improvement is required. However, by doing this, a person's positive qualities are often taken for granted or ignored. An inventory of what you do well can counterbalance this tendency. When making your inventory, include both work and non-work items. Your goal is to create a long list, so include everything you can think of and don't be too critical.

Finally, you must learn to deal with requests that come your way. Basically, you do this by learning to say "no" or at least to say, "later." When someone asks you to do something, question its priority or importance. Don't let your own judgment be overshadowed by the organizational rank or intensity of the person making the request. Compare the priority of the request to the priority of what you would otherwise be doing and use one of the following responses, as appropriate:

➤ "I can take care of that, but what I'm doing right now will be delayed. Is your request more important?

➤ "I'll be glad to handle that for you. However, I can't get to it until I finish what I'm doing. That will be…"

➤ "I'm sorry, I don't have time to take on any new work. I'll call you when my schedule frees up."

➤ "I appreciate your vote of confidence but just can't work it into my schedule at this time. Sorry."

➤ "I'm sorry, I just can't do it. Have you considered asking…"

Perfection

Some tasks require very high quality output. As such, spending extra time checking and rechecking to ensure nearly-perfect performance is justified. However, many things do not require that level of quality. The key is to distinguish between the ones requiring high quality and those that do not. Then, you can invest your time to achieve near-perfect results when required but won't waste time to attain perfection if it is unnecessary.

People who score low in this category (less than 10) may also waste time. Because of low quality standards, they may have to redo work that does not meet minimum standards of acceptability. Investing a little more time could result in substantial savings by eliminating the need to do something twice.

If this area is a problem for you, try the following techniques:

First, obtain a clear understanding of the quality level expected by the one assigning you the work. Ask questions like those below.

> ➤ Do you want a precise or an approximate answer?

> ➤ How much time and money can be spent to achieve a quality outcome?

> ➤ What quality level is expected?

> ➤ What is the cutoff on your range of acceptable quality?

Secondly, remember that time and effort invested in quality assurance should not exceed the costs of potential error. You need a positive return on investment. To achieve this, you need to estimate the cost of potential error. If it is low, you can't afford to spend a lot of time to eliminate all the errors. If the cost is high, you obviously should take the time.

The potential costs of perfection can be great. When standards are too high, there will be very few times when they are met. This often leads to disappointment due to infrequent opportunities to experience success. Constant disappointment can have a severe negative impact on people's attitude.

Risk Avoidance

People with a high need to avoid risk typically take more time studying and analyzing options, checking with others to obtain concurrence, and waiting (or hesitating) to take action. Again, there may be times when any or all of these time-consuming activities are justified, but a problem arises when there is a lack of differentiation based on some valid criterion.

If risk avoidance is a problem for you, try the following techniques:

First, examine what is at stake when you find yourself taking more time than justified before rendering a decision or taking action. What is at risk? What will happen if it doesn't work out? Will you be embarrassed? Will you get fired? Will someone be seriously injured? Will the company lose a lot of money?

Then, explore the question: What will happen if it *does* work out? Will you get what you want? Will you meet the deadline? Will you save the company money? Will it improve the business?

Finally, compare the potential payoff and the potential cost of the opportunity you face. Which is more likely to occur? Is the potential payoff worth the risk? If so, move forward with conviction. If not, abandon the idea and don't look back.

There simply is no way to eliminate all risk. It is a normal part of life brought about by an inability to foresee the future. Foolish action, obviously, is to be avoided, but calculated risks should be taken when there is a high probability of a positive outcome.

Environmental Time-Wasters

Even if you are well-organized and making effective use of time, there will always be interruptions and distractions from outside sources. Here are ideas for handling some of the most common ones.

Visitors

Controlling time taken up by visitors requires both courtesy and judgment. As a starting point, limit the number of people you invite to your work area. If you need to meet with a colleague at your facility, go to his or her work area. This way you can simply excuse yourself when your task is accomplished. It is often more difficult to get people to leave your area than it is for you to leave theirs.

Discourage drop-in visitors by turning your desk away from the door. When people see you are busy, they tend to not interrupt. Also, you might consider closing your door, if you have one, when you need to concentrate.

When someone unexpectedly drops in, stand up to talk. Don't invite your visitor to be seated unless you have the time. Usually, when you stand, your visitor will also stand. This should shorten the length of the visit. If this does not work, be honest and say something like, "Thanks for dropping in. You'll have to excuse me now because I need to get this project finished."

Telephone Calls

For many, telephone calls are a constant interruption. You cannot eliminate all of them. You can, however, limit the amount of time they take. If you are fortunate enough to have someone answer your phone, calls should be screened. Review which calls need a personal follow-up and delegate the others. Messages should be taken during periods when you do not wish to be interrupted.

When talking on the phone, limit social conversation. Provide short answers to questions. End the conversation, in a polite way, when it has achieved its business purpose.

Mail

A third distraction is your mail. Unsolicited mail arrives in an unending flood. If someone else sorts your mail, give some guidelines on what you want to see separated into piles:

➤ "information only" items

➤ "action" items

➤ items to route to others

➤ items to toss

Learn to handle each piece of mail *once*. As you read it, decide what action is required and then take that action, even if it is to put it into an action file. "Information only" mail can be saved and read at a more convenient time (e.g., while commuting or waiting for appointments, over lunch, or in the evening). You can save time by responding to some mail by telephone. If information is needed, it might be possible to have someone else telephone and pass on what is required. Another idea is to write a brief response in longhand on the original letter and mail it back. If a record is needed, photocopy it before it is mailed.

Waiting

We all spend too much time waiting–for appointments, for meetings to begin, for others to complete something, for airplanes, and as we commute. Opportunities exist to make better use of this waiting time.

"Waiting" time need not be *wasted* time. Two approaches will help: First, don't spend unreasonable time waiting for others with whom you have appointments. If you go to someone's office and are not received promptly, leave word with a secretary to call you when your party is ready and return to your office.

Second, make productive use of waiting time. For example, read your mail (including trade and professional journals), carry a tablet and pencil to develop plans or write letters, or carry a file of low-priority items to complete.

A compact cassette recorder can help improve your productivity during travel and commuting. Either listen to informational tapes or use the machine to record ideas and instructions for when you return to your office.

Meetings

Time wasted in meetings comes from two sources: the meetings you call and the meetings you attend.

When you call a meeting, plan what you want to accomplish. Keep attendees to a minimum number of appropriate people. Briefly explain your agenda and move directly to the purpose of the meeting. Establish a time limit. Keep the discussion on track by periodically summarizing where you are. When the business has been completed, assign responsibilities, and establish follow-up dates to convert decisions to action; then adjourn the meeting.

A common time-waster is the "regular staff meeting." Two suggestions can make significant improvements. First, set an agenda by asking, "What do we have to talk about today?" If more material is generated than can be handled in the available time, prioritize the list. If nothing significant is offered, adjourn the meeting. A second suggestion is to eliminate any discussion that involves only two participants. These should be handled as one-to-one sessions.

Before you attend someone else's meeting, make sure it is necessary for you to be there. If it is, arrive on time and be prepared to participate in the discussion. Avoid taking the discussion off track or prolonging it. Work to make the meeting productive. Add any follow-up items to your list of things to do, within appropriate priority designation.

Crises

Many people believe crises are unavoidable. That is only partly true. Unexpected events do occur and some must be handled then and there. Many crises, however, are recurring events brought on by something that either was or was not done. When you delay something that needs doing, you are helping to create a future crises.

A starting point to reduce future crises is to review past crises. Are there patterns? Often you can develop a response to recurring problems. For example, if there has been a regular breakdown of a particular piece of machinery, you can plan to respond to the next breakdown by replacement, having a standby available, etc.

Another way to reduce crises is through contingency planning. Study the key elements of a project: quality, quantity, cost, and timeliness. Then think through three questions so that you will be ready to respond when a crisis occurs:

➤ What is likely to go wrong?

➤ When will I know about it?

➤ What will I do about it?

Some crises are beyond your control. For example, you may have unrealistic deadlines laid on you, priorities may be changed at the last minute, people may make mistakes, or machines may break down. When this happens, take a deep breath and relax for a few minutes. Think through what needs to be done and consider the alternatives. Then approach the situation in an orderly, methodical way. You don't want to precipitate a second crisis by the way you handle the first one.

WHEN THINGS GO WRONG

There will be times when nothing you can do will prevent the worst from happening. If a deadline or quality standard is missed, here are some different solutions you can try to get back on track.

1 Renegotiate: The simplest action when you can't make a deadline is to renegotiate the due date. Perhaps there is enough flexibility that a day or two longer doesn't really matter.

2 Recover Lost Time During Later Steps: If, in the early stages of a project, a step takes longer than planned, reexamine time allocations for the remaining steps. Perhaps other time can be saved so that overall time on the project will not increase.

3 Narrow the Scope of the Project: Once underway you may find it will take longer than planned to accomplish everything you planned. When time is critical, you may have to eliminate some nonessential things to meet the deadline.

4 Deploy More Resources: You may need to put more people or machines on the project. This option clearly increases the cost, so it represents a decision that weighs the cost against the importance of the deadline.

5 **Accept Substitutions:** When a needed item is not available, you may be able to substitute a comparable item to meet your deadline.

6 **Seek Alternative Sources:** When a supplier you are depending upon cannot deliver within your time frame, look for other suppliers who can. (You may choose to pursue other sources before accepting substitutions.)

7 **Accept Partial Delivery:** Sometimes a supplier cannot deliver an entire order but can deliver the amount you need to get you past a critical point. After that, the remainder of the order can be delivered to everyone's satisfaction.

8 **Offer Incentives:** This option calls for going beyond the terms of an agreement to get someone you are dependent upon to put forth extra effort. It might be a bonus clause in a contract for on-time delivery, a penalty clause for late delivery, or simply buying someone lunch.

9 **Demand Compliance:** Sometimes it is necessary to stand up for your rights and demand delivery according to the agreement. Occasionally, an appeal to a higher authority will produce the desired results.

DEALING WITH TIME-WASTERS

Now that you have read about time-wasters and how to deal with them, take a few minutes to look at your own situation. List as many time-wasters you have experienced as you can.

List of Time-Wasters

Self-Generated	Environmental

1. From your list of time-wasters select the three most serious. What are they? How much time do they consume? What causes them?

   1. _____

   2. _____

   3. _____

2. List possible ways to reduce the impact of these time-wasters.

_____

_____

_____

CASE STUDY: THE PROGRAM REALLY WORKS

I have always admired how Bill does so much without seeming rushed. He always seems to have plenty of time when we talk. I know for a fact he rarely takes work home with him. I finally decided to ask Bill the secrets of his time management.

He began by saying he once had a real time management problem. Because of it he looked for ways to make better use of time. He read books on the subject and put some of their ideas into practice. Bill explained that the most important lesson he learned was to adapt techniques to his individual situation. He explained the following four basic concepts as keys to his success:

First, and most important, Bill said, he always looks ahead. He lists the goals he is working toward and has a plan to get there. He said he has learned to anticipate when things are due without waiting to be asked. As an example, budgets are due the second quarter every year. Bill does not wait until he receives a memo requesting his budget; rather, he works it into his schedule.

Second, he establishes priorities. There is always more to do than the time to complete it. Occasionally this may mean foregoing something he would like to do in favor of something that has to be done. When setting priorities, Bill said he takes into account his management's wishes as well as his judgment.

Third, Bill indicated, he learned to not try to do everything himself. He relies on his staff. Bill knows the people he can depend on and lets them do their job. He also trains others until he can rely on them.

Finally, he said, use only those techniques that help you. For example, he said he doesn't make a "things to do" list most days, because often his days are routine. However, when things begin to pile up, he always makes a list and starts at the top.

CONTINUED

Personal Time Management

According to Bill, that's it. Four basic ideas to help get better control over time:

1. Know your calendar

2. Prioritize demands on your time

3. Utilize the skills of others

4. Use techniques that help your unique situation

Case Study Questions

1. Do you think Bill's superiors see him as a good manager, and why?

   _____

   _____

2. How do you think Bill's staff feel about working for him, and why?

   _____

   _____

3. What did you learn from Bill's approach that could help you?

   _____

   _____

Five Tips for Effective Time Management

1 List and prioritize weekly objectives.

2 Make a daily "to do" list and prioritize it.

3 Devote primary attention to your A's.

4 Handle each piece of paper only once.

5 Continually ask, "What is the best use of my time right now?" and DO IT!

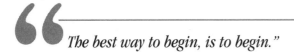

"The best way to begin, is to begin."

Marie Edmond Jones

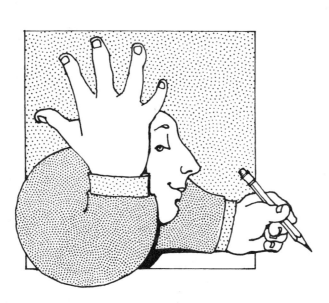

Time Management
Innovations

Telephone Enhancements

The electronics industry is developing new and improved products at such a rapid pace that it is difficult to keep up with the latest time-saving innovations. The telephone has been a standard part of office equipment since the turn of the 20th century. However, recent enhancements make it faster and easier to use.

Answering Machines

If you don't have one, you should consider getting one for the office, as well as at home. Answering machines allow you to receive calls and return them at your convenience. Newer models display the phone number from which the incoming call originated, so you can decide whether to take the call immediately or have it recorded. There are even portable models you can take with you and plug into the telephone jack in your hotel room. Some of these models double as dictating machines and alarm clocks. When buying an answering machine, select one that automatically records the date and time of calls and is accessible from any touch-tone phone for message retrieval.

Voicemail

Voicemail ties a telephone system and a computer together for greater capacity and enhanced operating features. You can change the outgoing message, retrieve incoming messages, and forward incoming messages from any touch-tone phone. In contrast to answering machine messages, voicemail messages should contain a complete message rather than a request for a return phone call.

Dialing Features

Some of the latest innovations have focused on reducing the time and effort of dialing. Many telephones have the capacity to store telephone numbers, which can then be dialed by pressing one or two buttons rather than the 10 numbers required to dial another area code. The newest feature is voice-activated dialing. These models store up to 50 names and respond to spoken commands. To dial Bill Jones, simply say "Bill Jones" into the speaker. There is also an electronic Rolodex on the market that stores up to 400 names, addresses, and phone numbers. You find the file you want by turning the rotary dial; then you press the automatic dial button to place your call.

Hands-free Operation

If you frequently refer to blueprints, maps, or papers while talking on the phone, it is much more convenient to have both hands free. Also, with your hands free, you can be doing other things while talking to someone or waiting on hold. Two features allow you this freedom: One is the speakerphone; the other is a headset. The speakerphone is in common use, but you may not have considered a headset. Today they are lightweight and extremely compact. If you make several calls during the day, a hands-free headset will reduce or eliminate sore ears and neck pain.

Call Forwarding

This feature permits you to program your phone to automatically forward calls to another phone. If you are going to have access to another phone, other than the one at your work station, you can take calls, and callers will never know that you are not at your regular location.

Computer Enhancements

Personal computers are as common today as typewriters were 40 years ago. As industry researchers continue to come up with new products, computers are getting smaller, have more features, and are more user-friendly. Here are a few of the latest contributions.

Portable Computers

The personal computer has been reduced in size to between six and seven pounds. Originally called laptop computers, today's models are called notebooks in recognition of their smaller size. These computers have all the features and capacity of a traditional desktop computer and are available with high-resolution color screens. The latest model comes with a built-in printer. Using the appropriate software, you send and receive email, can keep records of your travel expenses, and submit orders by cellular modem or fax. Traditional spreadsheet and word processing software allow you to analyze data and write reports while you travel or attend class.

Modems

Although not as new as some of the other features, modems are not as widely used as they could be. A modem connects your computer to others through the telephone system. This allows you to transmit and receive information. By using a service like CompuServe or Prodigy, you can browse through airline schedules and book your own travel arrangements, including hotel and rental car reservations. You can have access to stock exchange transactions and handle your own stock market trades. By using electronic bulletin board services, you can exchange information with anyone interested. You can communicate online with anyone who has the same service.

Scanners

Scanners import printed or graphic material from a page to your computer. There are hand-held and tabletop models available that work in either black-and-white or color. These are terrific time savers when you have to edit and update training manuals, policy manuals, or procedure guides. They also come in handy when you want to include pictures and graphics in a report or newsletter.

Speech Recognizers

Automatic Speech Recognition (ASR) uses a microphone for speech input and a microcomputer that processes voice data. Current models have a limited capacity of several hundred words. These devices take your spoken words and convert them through your word processor to printed words. This eliminates the need to transcribe dictated material from a tape recorder.

Electronic Notepads

These hand-held computers use an electronic pen (called a stylus) for entering data. The computer understands printing and symbols the same way other computers understand keyboard and mouse commands. These devices come in handy for taking notes in the field or in meetings.

Electronic Organizers

Small enough to tuck into a pocket or briefcase, electronic organizers keep track of your schedule and store telephone numbers, addresses, and important dates. Many also have a built-in calculator and clock. Some store notes that you type into memory, remind you to do things and provide foreign language translation, a dictionary, a thesaurus, and a calendar through the year 9999. Some models can send faxes and have computer games; some even accept handwritten input the same as electronic notepads.

Personal Digital Assistants (PDAs)

Besides having larger memory than electronic notepads and an almost limitless capability for expansion and add-ons (voice recorders, digital cameras, scanners, games, word processing and spreadsheet software) as a desktop computer. PDAs also have the capability to be "hot-synced" with your main computer at home or at work. This means that with the push of a button you can transfer information from your computer to your PDA or from your PDA to your computer instantly. You can share, transfer, and even back-up your files. These palm-sized machines are becoming the industry standard for time, resource, and contact management.

Other Technological Enhancements

You can often save time when you are away from your telephone, by staying in contact with your workplace. Here are some common ways to stay in touch.

Pagers

These little gadgets that you clip on to your belt, carry in a pocket or purse, or wear on your wrist have been around for 40 years or so. But they have come a long way from the original model where a beep was a signal to call in. Today some models will store up to 10 numbers for you to call back. Others display brief messages. The most sophisticated systems link to satellites to contact you anywhere in the country. The number of pagers in use grew from 19.2 million at the end of 1993 to 33 million by 1997 and continues to grow each year.

Mobile or Cellular Phones

If you spend a lot of time in a car, a mobile phone can be both a convenience and a time-saver. Portable phones keep you in touch wherever you are. The attaché case models with their own battery packs provide longer service and are more accessible. Pocket models need frequent battery recharging, and you may find some areas where you can't be reached. Portable phones allow you to be productive during both waiting and travel time. The latest innovations are web phones that allow you to check your email and access the Internet in addition to serving as a phone and a pager.

Fax Machines

One of the greatest time savers in the array of electronic innovations is the fax machine. This machine transmits written or graphic text over telephone systems. As a result, it provides immediate delivery of written material. With their ease of operation and inexpensive price, nearly every company and many homes have fax machines. Most machines can be programmed to transmit during the hours of lowest telephone rates. They also will simultaneously send a message to a list of recipients. DHL Worldwide Express offers a service combining facsimile transmission and courier deliver. Fax your message to them, and they will send it via satellite, print it, and deliver it almost anywhere in the world. Some of the more popular, low-cost machines combine the features of a telephone, an answering machine, and a fax machine. There is a portable machine available that weighs $5\frac{1}{2}$ pounds, holds 30 sheets of letter-size paper, and doubles as a copier. With the right software, you can even send faxes directly from your computer.

Meeting Alternatives

Meetings cost a lot of time and money, especially if attendees come from different locations. Occasionally, rather than calling a meeting, consider one of these alternatives.

Conference Telephone Calls

With the assistance of an operator, you can have several people connected to the same telephone conversation. This allows discussion among all participants. Typically, conference calls should be scheduled in advance in order to ensure reaching everyone.

Teleconferencing

Teleconferencing differs from conference telephone calls by tying two or more meetings together rather than tying three or more people together. A typical teleconference setup has people meet in a room equipped with voice-activated speakers. There can be up to 58 national or international locations tied together. Each location can go offline to hold a sub-meeting and then come back online to discuss results with others.

Videoconferencing

One-way video with two-way audio is the most common form of video-conferencing currently in use because of the high cost of video transmission. However, this could soon change with new technology. At the present time, you can transmit from a specially equipped conference room or studio, and remote locations can receive video on a regular television monitor. Remote meeting rooms can be equipped for voice communication among them and with the central transmission point.

Saving Time on the Internet

If you have ever spent more than a few minutes on the Internet, you probably have been frustrated by the time it takes for websites to download to your browser. You have also probably grown weary of wading through the garbage search results to find the information you want. You may even be less-than-excited about email, if it slows you down with unsolicited, time-consuming messages, or junk mail. Here are some ideas to help you cope with these frustrations.

Internet Access

The determining factor of connection speed is the way you access the Internet. Common telephone lines are the most widely-used, but they are also the slowest. Broadband residential connection is coming into more use and promises to greatly increase the speed of data transmission between your computer and the Internet. This broadband service comes from three sources:

1. Companies that offer Digital Subscriber (DSL) service through existing phone lines. This service is typically eight times faster than most telephone line service. Unfortunately, this service is not yet available in all areas.

2. Cable TV companies that offer cable-modem service. This service can be faster than DSL, but the speed decreases as more people in a given area go online. This may become the dominant service since cable TV is so widely available.

3. Satellite TV companies that offer connections through their dishes. This service provides high-speed transmission for outgoing data but relies on existing telephone lines for incoming data.

Hardware

Computer hardware also affects the speed of your Internet service. Your modem, computer processor, and hard drive storage may be causing the bottlenecks in your system. If you suspect your hardware is holding you back, consult a computer technician.

Software

There are several web utilities available that will increase your Internet efficiency. Here are a few to consider:

Ad Filter Programs

These utilities dramatically increase your connection speed by blocking banners, ads, and pop-up windows so that you only view the core content of a page. They remove blinking/animated text, embedded ads, and background music as well as shield your browsing habits from advertisers.

Multi-Engine Searches

Using a search engine that draws on several search engines simultaneously will save time and produce better results. With more than 10 search engines on the Internet, it is nearly impossible to know which one will be best for a given search. These utilities are available for purchase or you can use ones available online.

Email Tools

Filters

The starting place for gaining control is to use a program that filters out all of the junk email before you see it and waste your time on it. The great thing about these filters is that you can also filter newsletters into specific folders to be read when you have time. If you have an assistant, you could have your emails pre-screened.

Separate Accounts

It is much more efficient if you don't mix personal and business messages. If your Internet Service Provider (ISP) does not accommodate multiple email addresses, use the paid service for business and set up a free email service for your personal messages.

Email Address Book

Use the address book provided by your email program, rather than retyping each address. It is both more convenient and more accurate. You can also use the address book to set up distribution lists if you routinely send messages to a group.

Organize Your Email

As soon as you've read or acted upon an email message, file it into its specific folder. This will eliminate rereading messages and unclutter your inbox.

Other Useful Tips

Customize Your Start Page

Most browsers and service providers allow you to customize your start (or "home") page so you can have the most-used links, news, and other information you want at your fingertips. Most browsers have appointment calendars and reminders as well.

Focus Your Search

When you need to find something on the Internet, often you will find yourself off track if you do not remain focused on what you are looking for. Avoid following any link that does not directly relate to your end goal.

Use Bookmarks

Bookmarking the websites you visit saves you from having to retype an entire URL every time you want to view a web page. Organize your bookmarks into folders by subject, and arrange them so the frequently used ones are at the top. Delete inactive or unused bookmarks to save space.

Read Offline

If you read a lot of material from websites, download the pages to your hard drive to be read at your leisure. You can even print them and take them with you while commuting or waiting for appointments, saving you from having to absorb online material immediately.

EVALUATE YOUR USE OF THE
LATEST ELECTRONIC TECHNOLOGY

Place a check (✔) by the items you are currently using and an X (✘) by the ones you want to investigate for possible use.

❏ answering machine	❏ voicemail
❏ automatic dialing	❏ email
❏ call forwarding	❏ voice-activated dialing
❏ cellular phone	❏ pager
❏ conference calls	❏ teleconferencing
❏ fax machine	❏ videoconferencing
❏ portable (laptop) computer	❏ information service
❏ scanner	❏ speech recognizer
❏ electronic organizer or PDA	❏ caller-ID
❏ modem	❏ hands-free headset

How do you see the items you are interested in saving you time?

_____

_____

_____

If you are not using the latest technology, what can you do to change the situation?

_____

_____

_____

PART 4

Time-Saving Tips for Travelers

Plan Your Travel Wisely

Is This Trip Necessary?

Business travel can consume a great deal of time. Because of this, it presents opportunities to save time by examining current habits and finding better ways. Some of these tips will also be helpful for personal travel.

Before booking your flight, make sure the trip is necessary. Some options to consider are: Can you handle it by mail or telephone? Can the person you plan to visit come see you? Can someone else go in your place? When you consider these options, you may find you can save time simply by *not* making the trip.

If you must make the trip, carefully plan the details. Start by writing your objectives. (What do you hope to accomplish?) Then, make an agenda for your meeting that will lead to achieving your objectives. Next, make a specific appointment with the person or people you plan to visit. Follow up with a written confirmation of the appointment and a copy of your agenda. Then, upon arrival at your destination, reconfirm your appointment by telephone.

If you have several appointments, plan your schedule to minimize travel distance between them. And be sure to leave enough time to get from one meeting to the next. You can't always depend on finding a taxi or a parking space.

Choose the Best Mode of Travel

Although airplanes are the most common mode of business travel, don't overlook the advantages of traveling by car or train when circumstances permit.

If it is 200 miles or less to your destination, consider driving. It will probably save you time when you consider the time spent in getting to the airport, parking your car, flying to your destination, and getting a taxi or rental car to get to your appointment. If you don't have a company car, consider renting one for the trip rather than using your personal car.

Another option often overlooked is to travel by train. There is excellent train service in many parts of the world, and you typically arrive in the central business district of a city, eliminating a long taxi or rental car trip into town.

If you have a company travel department or a contract travel agent, you will be expected to make your arrangements through them. However, if these services are not available, you can work through the travel agent of your choice or call airlines and hotels directly on toll-free reservation phone lines or use online booking services. Here are some time saving tips when booking air travel.

➤ Try to book a direct, non-stop flight. Not only will your in-flight time be less, but you will reduce the chances of delayed departures.

➤ Obtain boarding passes when you pick up your tickets. This eliminates waiting in line at the airport for a seat assignment.

➤ Always get information on flights that are both earlier and later than your scheduled departure. Then, if your plans change or your flight is delayed or canceled, you will know what options are available.

➤ Ask for the on-time ratings of flights you are considering. This figure is readily available and will tell you the percentage of time the flight has arrived on schedule during the past two months.

➤ Avoid Friday travel whenever possible. This is the industry's busiest day during a typical week.

➤ Avoid departures between 6:30 A.M. and 10:00 A.M., if possible. Mid-afternoons are the slowest times.

If you, or someone in your office, must handle your travel arrangements, here are three sources of valuable information. Any one of them can save you both time and money:

➤ Several websites let you use your personal computer and modem to book flights, hotels, and car rentals at the best available prices. You can handle everything via your computer (including meal choice and seat assignment) and have tickets and confirmations mailed to you.

➤ VTS Travel Enterprises will save you time and money by researching airfares and hotel rates. After you call, they check and recheck for the lowest rates right up to your scheduled departure. If a better price becomes available for the same flight and hotel, they automatically book it and cancel your previous reservation.

➤ Best Fares magazine publishes a monthly list of airfares, hotel and rental car discounts, and other helpful travel information. Their travel club gives an 8 percent rebate on tickets and charges an $8 handling fee. They offer 25% discounts on international travel.

Make the Most of Travel Time

The best way to save time at check-in is to bypass the process as much as possible. With your ticket, boarding pass, and carry-on luggage only, you can go directly to the boarding gate check-in counter, thus avoiding long lines at the regular counter.

Plan your wardrobe so that you can get by with carry-on luggage only. Since most airlines have a restriction of two carry-on items, the typical garment bag, briefcase, and suitcase present a challenge. One option is to carry a small portfolio rather than a briefcase and put it in either your suitcase or a side pocket of your garment bag. Or you can consolidate your garment bag and suitcase.

If you must have more luggage than you can carry on, use curbside check-in. Or, if you qualify by the level of your frequent flyer program or are traveling first class or business class, use the special counter available to you. Because of the potential for lost luggage, always carry the minimum of toiletries and personal items with you.

Waiting and In-Flight Time

You can recognize seasoned business travelers. They are the ones who make full use of their time in waiting lounges and on the aircraft. To make best use of your time, take along work that can be handled without reference to bulky files. This can include such things as proofreading, catching up on correspondence, and reading reports, books, and magazines.

There is a selection of portable office equipment that will help save you time. Laptop computers are very popular today among business travelers. You can take advantage of a variety of software or just use it as a word processor. Also, tape recorders and dictating machines are handy for dictating correspondence, reports, ideas, and suggestions that occur to you as you travel. In-flight telephone service can keep you in touch with your office or clients and you can even send and receive email while in the air.

Listening to your own audiotapes of business books or other training material can be much more rewarding than listening to airline music or watching a movie.

Getting to and from the Airport

In most cities, you can travel to and from the airport by private car, taxi, bus or van, limousine, or rental car. At their home city, many people choose to drive their own car. This may be the best choice; but consider the convenience of parking at both your workplace and the airport. Also consider the availability of other modes of transportation to get you to either your home or workplace when you return. You may find another choice will save you time.

When you arrive at your destination, limousine service is the most convenient. The driver will be waiting for you, help you with your luggage, and deliver you to your hotel. Taxi service can also be convenient, but there may be a considerable wait at busy airports. Bus and van service usually involve a delay as you must wait for the van to fill up or the bus to operate on schedule.

All of these choices leave you without transportation after you have been dropped at your hotel. You must either walk or rely on taxi service for local travel. A rental car is more convenient if your trip calls for much local travel. To save time at the car rental counter, have a confirmed reservation. Most rental companies gather and store in their computer all the information they need. With this information on file and a confirmed reservation, you can bypass the check-in counter and go directly to pick up your car. When you return, use the express check-in system to avoid waiting in line.

Saving Time at Your Hotel

Most of the major hotel chains are offering extra services geared to the business traveler. Take advantage of these services plus these other ideas to save time:

➤ Find the most convenient hotel. Ask the person you are visiting for suggestions, or have your travel agent check the hotels near the address you will be visiting. If several people are flying in for a meeting, consider booking accommodations for everyone at an airport hotel.

➤ Confirm your reservation with a credit card and get a confirmation number in writing or make a note of it over the phone.

➤ Book your room on the executive floor if your frequent traveler program membership permits, you have upgrade coupons, or your travel budget can handle it. The additional amenities often include newspapers, light breakfasts, extra service people, and use of office equipment such as fax machines and typewriters.

➤ Streamline your check out by calling up your bill on the television screen and reviewing it for accuracy. At most hotels, you will receive a copy of your bill under the door on the morning of your departure. If so, you simply drop off your key on the way out. Checking your bill the night before helps ensure that everything will be in order.

Put Your Travel Plans in Writing

After all arrangements have been made, write up an itinerary of your trip. Include the names of people you will be visiting with their addresses, phone and fax numbers. Include the date and time of each appointment. Show the date and time of departure and arrival along with flight or train numbers. Also, show the name, address, and telephone number of the hotel where you will be staying along with your confirmation number.

This information should be given to family members, office staff, and anyone else who might need to contact you for business or personal reasons. (It will also be helpful to take a copy with you.)

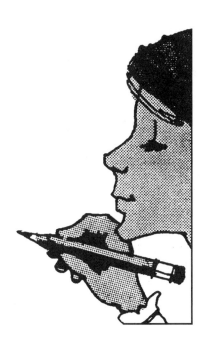

TRAVELER'S CHECKLIST OF TIME-SAVING TIPS

➤ Is this trip really necessary?

➤ Do you have written objectives and an agenda?

➤ Do you have a confirmed appointment?

➤ Have you chosen the best mode of travel?

➤ Have you booked the most direct flight?

➤ Have you avoided Friday travel?

➤ Have you avoided early morning travel?

➤ Do you have your tickets and boarding passes?

➤ Do you know the flights before and after yours?

➤ Can you carry on all of your luggage?

➤ Have you arranged the best ground transportation?

➤ Have you booked the most convenient hotel?

➤ Do you have sufficient work to stay busy?

➤ Do you have the equipment you may need?

➤ Have you advised everyone of your travel plans?

Action

Planning

Applying What You've Learned

This section contains worksheets which will help you apply time management principles and techniques to your own situation. To complete this section, you need to do the following:

1 **Gather Data:** Keep a daily time log for one week similar to the one shown on page 101. This will provide accurate information for you to improve your use of time. Be honest—and attentive—to detail.

2 **Analyze Your Use of Time:** Working with the data gathered, analyze your current use of time. List opportunities for improvement.

3 **Develop Action Plans:** From your analysis, develop specific action plans to bring about the desired improvement in your use of time.

4 **Follow-Up:** Six weeks after beginning your time management improvement effort, complete the Progress Survey shown on page 107 to assess your progress, and determine what work still needs to be done.

Keeping a Daily Time Log

➤ Select a typical week. Avoid weeks with vacation, sick leave, personal leave, holidays, etc.

➤ Record activities at least every half-hour. Be specific. For example, identify visitors and record the duration and topics of conversations. (Be honest. Only you will have access to this information.)

➤ Write a comment on each activity. Did something take longer than usual? Why? Were you interrupted?

➤ At the end of the day note whether this day was typical, busier than usual, or less busy than usual. Add up time spent on various major activities (meetings, visitors, telephoning, mail, etc.), and show totals along with other comments at the bottom of the Daily Time Log.

See next page for a sample Daily Time Log.

DAILY TIME LOG

Day of Week: M   T   W   T   F

Time	Activity	Comments
7:00		
7:30		
8:00		
8:30		
9:00		
9:30		
10:00		
10:30		
11:00		
11:30		
12:00		
12:30		
1:00		
1:30		
2:00		
2:30		
3:00		
3:30		
4:00		
4:30		
5:00		
5:30		

Was this day   ❏   Typical?   Comments: _____

                ❏   More busy?   _____

                ❏   Less busy?   _____

Photocopy this form for each day of the week.

TIME ANALYZER

Using your time log as a basis, draw conclusions and record your responses to the following questions.

1. Which part of each day was most productive? Which was least productive? Why?

   _____

   _____

2. What are the recurring patterns of inefficiency (e.g., waiting for something, searching for something, or interruption)?

   _____

   _____

3. What do you do that may not be necessary? (Be liberal since this list is simply for further review later.)

   _____

   _____

4. What do you do that may be inappropriate? (Again, these are only prospects for further scrutiny.)

   _____

   _____

5. Where are your opportunities for increased efficiency?

   _____

   _____

6. On what occasions do you allow enjoyment to override a priority task?

   _____

   _____

7. Which activities do not contribute to achieving one of your objectives? How can you change this?

   _____

   _____

8. On average, what percentage of work time are you productive?_____

9. What is your reaction to this figure? (Be honest.)

   _____

   _____

Planning for Improved Time Utilization

There are five steps you can take to make the best use of your available time.

1 **State your time improvement objective.** Be specific in terms of both how much time you hope to free up in your weekly schedule and the target date by which you hope to accomplish it.

_____

_____

_____

2 **Identify your areas of opportunity.** Be specific in what tasks might be eliminated or reassigned. What time-wasters can be eliminated or reduced? What planning needs to be done?

	Opportunity	Estimated Time Savings
1.	_____	_____
2.	_____	_____
3.	_____	_____
4.	_____	_____
5.	_____	_____
6.	_____	_____
7.	_____	_____
8.	_____	_____
9.	_____	_____
10.	_____	_____

3 **Select those opportunities you plan to pursue.** Add up the anticipated time savings and compare it with your targeted time savings. (Space is provided for planning three opportunities. If you have more, photocopy as many additional pages as you need.)

Opportunity No. 1: _____

_____

_____

Action Steps	Target Dates
_____	_____
_____	_____
_____	_____
_____	_____
_____	_____
_____	_____
_____	_____
_____	_____
_____	_____
_____	_____
_____	_____
_____	_____
_____	_____
_____	_____
_____	_____
_____	_____

Opportunity No. 2: _____

_____

_____

Action Steps	**Target Dates**
_____	_____
_____	_____
_____	_____
_____	_____
_____	_____
_____	_____
_____	_____
_____	_____

Opportunity No. 3: _____

_____

_____

Action Steps	**Target Dates**
_____	_____
_____	_____
_____	_____
_____	_____
_____	_____
_____	_____
_____	_____
_____	_____

4 **List others who need to be involved when implementing your changes.** This should include review and approval by your manager as well as the agreement and cooperation of those who may assume part of your duties and responsibilities.

Name   **Position**

_____   _____

_____   _____

_____   _____

_____   _____

_____   _____

5 **Follow up in 30 days.** Review your progress and repeat any steps that have not provided the results you anticipated.

Summarize your progress:

_____

_____

_____

What has interfered with your progress?

_____

_____

_____

How can you overcome these problems?

_____

_____

_____

PROGRESS SURVEY

Six weeks after beginning your time management improvement effort, complete the following survey. It will show where you are doing well and where you still need to devote attention.

Yes = 1   Usually = 2   Sometimes = 3   Rarely = 4
Never or No = 5   Not Applicable = NA

_____ 1. Do you have a clearly-defined list of written objectives?

_____ 2. Do you plan and schedule your time on a weekly and daily basis?

_____ 3. Can you find large blocks of uninterrupted time when you need to?

_____ 4. Have you reduced or eliminated recurring crises form your job?

_____ 5. Do you refuse to answer the phone when engaged in important conversations or activities?

_____ 6. Do you use travel and waiting time productively?

_____ 7. Do you delegate as much as possible?

_____ 8. Do you prevent your staff from delegating their tasks and decision making to you?

_____ 9. Do you take time each day to think about what you are doing relative to what you are trying to accomplish?

_____ 10. Have you eliminated any time-wasters during the past week?

_____ 11. Do you feel in control of your time?

_____ 12. Are your desk and office well-organized and free of clutter?

_____ 13. Have you reduced or eliminated time wasted in meetings?

_____ 14. Have you conquered your tendency to procrastinate?

_____ 15. Do you carry out work on the basis of your priorities?

CONTINUED

_____ 16. Do you resist the temptation to get overly involved in nonproductive activities?

_____ 17. Do you control your schedule so that others do not waste time waiting for you?

_____ 18. Do you meet your deadlines?

_____ 19. Can you identify the critical few tasks that account for the majority of your results?

_____ 20. Are you better organized and accomplishing more than you were six weeks ago?

_____ 21. Have you been able to reduce the amount of time you spend on routine paperwork?

_____ 22. Do you effectively control interruptions and drop-in visitors?

_____ 23. Have you mastered the ability to say "No" whenever you should?

_____ 24. Do you stay current with your most important reading?

_____ 25. Did you leave enough time for yourself (recreation, study, community service, family)?

_____ **TOTAL**

Scoring: Add the points assigned to each item. The lower your score, the better. Look particularly at items you rated 4 or 5. These represent challenges for further development.

This survey should be taken quarterly as old habits have a way of recurring.

Conclusion

Time Management in a Nutshell

Congratulations on completing this program. We hope it was an effective use of your time!

Nearly everyone has the potential to save five to 10 hours a week. To do so requires discipline and a commitment to the basic principles in this book.

In review, you need to identify the portion of time over which you have control. Then develop procedures for repetitive operations and make use of available technology. You should concentrate on high-payoff activities.

Also, identify and make best use of your personal energy cycle. Use prime time to handle work requiring concentration. If possible, arrange for a quiet period to match your prime time when there are pressing matters.

Next, establish quarterly objectives and construct plans to accomplish them. Maintain some flexibility to respond to unexpected events. Prioritize the action steps required to achieve your objectives.

Analyze your use of time. Keep a time log for a typical week then examine your activities using the tests of necessity, appropriateness, and efficiency. From this examination will come the essential elements of your job so you can isolate time-wasters and deal with them.

Finally, remember that the ideas in this book must be adapted to fit your unique situation. Modify the worksheets if necessary, develop your own personal file system, utilize electronic equipment available to you, and use the planning techniques when appropriate. Don't let the use of forms and procedures distract you from doing your job.

Keep this program handy for reference. To check your progress, make a note to review the book again in three months.

Good luck!

Additional Reading

Bly, Robert W. *101 Ways to Make Every Second Count*. Hawthorne, NJ: Career Press, 1999.

Covey, Stephen R. *First Things First: Every Day*. NY: Fireside Books, 1994.

Douglass, Merrill E. *ABC Time Tips*. NY: McGraw-Hill, 1998.

Ferner, Jack D. *Successful Time Management*. NY: John Wiley & Sons, 1995.

Haynes, Marion E. *Practical Time Management*. Menlo Park, CA: Crisp Learning, 1991.

Lakein, Alan. *How to Get Control of Your Time and Your Life*. Np: New American Library, 1996.

LeBoeuf, Michael. *Working Smart: How to Accomplish More in Half the Time*. NY: Warner Books, 1993.

MacKenzie, R. Alec. *The Time Trap: How to Get More Done in Less Time*. NY: AMACOM, 1997.

Materka, Pat Roessle. *Time In, Time Out, Time Enough: A Time Management Guide for Women*. Englewood Cliffs, NJ: Prentice Hall, 1993.

Yager, Jan. *Creative Time Management for the New Millennium*. Stamford, CT: Hannacroix Creek Books, 1999.

NOTES

NOTES

Now Available From

CRISP.
Learning

Books • Videos • CD-ROMs • Computer-Based Training Products

Subject Areas Include:

Management
Human Resources
Communication Skills
Personal Development
Marketing/Sales
Organizational Development
Customer Service/Quality
Computer Skills
Small Business and Entrepreneurship
Adult Literacy and Learning
Life Planning and Retirement

CRISP WORLDWIDE DISTRIBUTION

English language books are distributed worldwide. Major international distributors include:

ASIA/PACIFIC

Australia/New Zealand: In Learning, PO Box 1051, Springwood QLD, Brisbane,
Australia 4127   Tel: 61-7-3-841-2286, Facsimile: 61-7-3-841-1580
ATTN: Messrs. Gordon

Philippines: National Book Store Inc., Quad Alpha Centrum Bldg, 125 Pioneer Street,
Mandaluyong, Metro Manila, Philippines   Tel: 632-631-8051, Facsimile: 632-631-5016

Singapore, Malaysia, Brunei, Indonesia: Times Book Shops. Direct sales HQ:
STP Distributors, Pasir Panjang Distrientre, Block 1 #03-01A, Pasir Panjang Rd,
Singapore 118480   Tel: 65-2767626, Facsimile: 65-2767119

Japan: Phoenix Associates Co., Ltd., Mizuho Bldng, 3-F, 2-12-2, Kami Osaki,
Shinagawa-Ku, Tokyo 141   Tel: 81-33-443-7231, Facsimile: 81-33-443-7640
ATTN: Mr. Peter Owans

CANADA

Crisp Learning Canada, 60 Briarwood Avenue, Mississauga, ON L5G 3N6 Canada
Tel: (905) 274-5678, Facsimile: (905) 278-2801
ATTN: Mr. Steve Connolly/Mr. Jerry McNabb

Trade Book Stores: Raincoast Books, 8680 Cambie Street,
Vancouver, BC V6P 6M9 Canada
Tel: (604) 323-7100, Facsimile: (604) 323-2600   ATTN: Order Desk

EUROPEAN UNION

England: Flex Training, Ltd., 9-15 Hitchin Street,
Baldock, Hertfordshire, SG7 6A, England
Tel: 44-1-46-289-6000, Facsimile: 44-1-46-289-2417   ATTN: Mr. David Willetts

INDIA

Multi-Media HRD, Pvt., Ltd., National House,
Tulloch Road, Appolo Bunder, Bombay, India 400-039
Tel: 91-22-204-2281, Facsimile: 91-22-283-6478   ATTN: Messrs. Aggarwal

SOUTH AMERICA

Mexico: Grupo Editorial Iberoamerica, Nebraska 199, Col. Napoles, 03810 Mexico, D.F.
Tel: 525-523-0994, Facsimile: 525-543-1173   ATTN: Señor Nicholas Grepe

SOUTH AFRICA

Alternative Books, PO Box 1345, Ferndale 2160, South Africa
Tel: 27-11-792-7730, Facsimile: 27-11-792-7787   ATTN: Mr. Vernon de Haas